easy OPENWORK knit tops™

Kennita Tully

Annie's®

Introduction

I chose these designs with the emerging knitter in mind, but I believe they will appeal to many seasoned knitters as well. The garments feature a variety of techniques, ranging from the basic garter or stockinette stitch, as a foundation for fine yarns and larger needles, to asymmetrical shaping and uneven hemlines.

Most of the designs I've chosen use yarn overs to create the openwork, often one of the first techniques new knitters are introduced to. Yarn overs form the basis for more intricate lacework and are a great place to start when you are ready to branch out and learn new stitches.

The stitch patterns I've used in this collection are simple and easy to memorize. The shaping is also minimal, making them an easy choice for beginners.

Drape and comfort are important to me when choosing projects, so I carefully chose yarns for these designs with drape in mind. If you substitute yarns, please do a large enough swatch to determine the drape.

Openwork is a wonderful way to show off your knits!

Kennita

Kennita Tully

Table of Contents

....

Star Mesh, page 5

Captivating Mesh Duo, page 19

Sheer Comfort, page 9

Star Mesh

You'll be sure to stand out in this soft and silky front-drape design!

· ·

Gauge
17 sts and 28 rows = 4 inches/10cm in Star Rib Mesh pat.

To save time, take time to check gauge.

Special Abbreviation
Centered Double Decrease (CDD): Slip next 2 sts as if to k2tog, k1, p2sso.

Pattern Stitch
Star Rib Mesh (multiple of 4 sts + 3)

Row 1 (WS): Purl.

Row 2: K2, *yo, CDD, yo, k1; rep from * to last st, k1.

Row 3: Purl.

Row 4: K1, ssk, yo, k1, *yo, CDD, yo, k1; rep from * to last 3 sts, yo, k2tog, k1.

Rep Rows 1–4 for pat.

Pattern Notes
Make and block a swatch in Star Rib Mesh pattern before beginning to be sure gauge is correct.

Circular needle is used to accommodate large number of stitches. Do not join; work back and forth in rows.

Use long-tail cast-on method throughout.

Needles with sharp points are recommended when working this stitch pattern.

Sleeve increases are worked 1 stitch in from the edge. Work increased stitches in Stockinette stitch until there are enough stitches to work another repeat of the pattern.

Back
Cast on 71 (79, 87, 95, 103, 111) sts.

Work Star Rib Mesh pat for 154 (162, 168, 176, 182, 190) rows or until back measures 22 (23, 24, 25, 26, 27) inches.

Bind off all sts on next RS row.

Mark center 6¾ (7, 7½, 7¾, 8¼, 8½) inches on top edge of piece to indicate back neck.

Front
Cast on 143 (159, 175, 191, 207, 223) sts.

Work Star Rib Mesh pat until front measures same as back.

Bind off all sts on next RS row.

Sleeve
Cast on 35 (35, 39, 39, 43, 43) sts.

Work Star Rib Mesh pat, inc 1 st each side [every 8 (6, 6, 6, 6, 4) rows] 13 (4, 6, 15, 17, 10) times, then [every 10 (8, 8, 8, 8, 6) rows] 3 (14, 12, 5, 3, 14) times—67 (71, 75, 79, 83, 91) sts.

Work even for 10 (8, 8, 6, 8, 6) more rows—144 (144, 140, 136, 134, 130) rows or until sleeve measures 20½ (20½, 20, 19½, 19, 18½) inches.

Bind off all sts on next RS row.

Finishing

Weave in ends.

Block to measurements.

Sew left shoulder seam from shoulder edge to neck edge.

Twist front piece so that lower right cast-on edge meets right shoulder.

Note: WS of front will be on outside of garment and drape will form at center front.

Sew right shoulder seam from shoulder edge to neck edge.

Center top of sleeves along shoulder edges and sew in place.

Sew underarm and side seams. ●

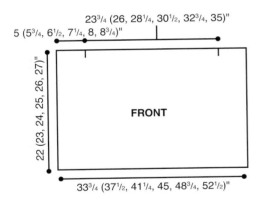

23³/₄ (26, 28¹/₄, 30¹/₂, 32³/₄, 35)"

5 (5³/₄, 6¹/₂, 7¹/₄, 8, 8³/₄)"

22 (23, 24, 25, 26, 27)"

FRONT

33³/₄ (37¹/₂, 41¹/₄, 45, 48³/₄, 52¹/₂)"

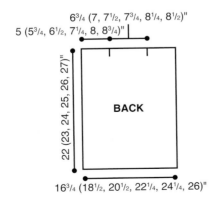

6³/₄ (7, 7¹/₂, 7³/₄, 8¹/₄, 8¹/₂)"

5 (5³/₄, 6¹/₂, 7¹/₄, 8, 8³/₄)"

22 (23, 24, 25, 26, 27)"

BACK

16³/₄ (18¹/₂, 20¹/₂, 22¹/₄, 24¹/₄, 26)"

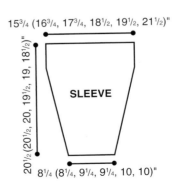

15³/₄ (16³/₄, 17³/₄, 18¹/₂, 19¹/₂, 21¹/₂)"

20¹/₂ (20¹/₂, 20, 19¹/₂, 19, 18¹/₂)"

SLEEVE

20¹/₂ (20¹/₂...

8¹/₄ (8¹/₄, 9¹/₄, 9¹/₄, 10, 10)"

Sheer Comfort

This super-meshy vest is made with a fine lace-weight yarn made from stainless steel! It knits up quicker than you think on a size 6 needle.

Skill Level

 EASY

Sizes

Woman's small (medium, large, X-large, 2X-large, 3X-large)

Instructions are given for smallest size, with larger sizes in parentheses. When only 1 number is given, it applies to all sizes.

Finished Measurements

Chest: 38 (42, 46, 50, 54, 58) inches
Length: 20 (21, 22, 23, 24, 25½) inches

Materials

- Habu Textiles Wool Stainless Steel (lace weight; 75% wool/25% stainless steel; 274 yds/14g per cone): 7 (8, 9, 10, 11, 12) cones bordeaux #49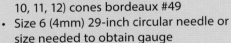
- Size 6 (4mm) 29-inch circular needle or size needed to obtain gauge
- Extra size 6 (4mm) needle (for 3-needle bind-off)
- Removable stitch marker
- Stitch holders

Gauge

20 sts and 36 rows = 4 inches/10cm in garter st with 2 strands of yarn held tog.

16 sts and 18 rows = 4 inches/10cm in Garter Drop St with 2 strands of yarn held tog.

To save time, take time to check gauge.

Pattern Stitch

Garter Drop St

Row 1: *K1, [yo] twice; rep from *, end k1.

Row 2: Knit all sts, dropping yo's.

Row 3: Knit.

Rep Rows 1–3 for pat.

Pattern Notes

Circular needle is used to accommodate large number of stitches. Do not join; work back and forth in rows.

Vest is worked with 2 strands of yarn held together throughout.

Needles with sharp points are recommended for use with stainless steel wool yarn.

To decrease at end of a row, work until 3 stitches remain, k2tog, k1.

To decrease at beginning of a row, k1, ssk, work to end.

When working the Garter Drop Stitch, pull the dropped stitches to elongate them before working Row 3 of pattern.

Vest

With 2 strands of yarn held tog, cast on 173 (193, 213, 233, 253, 273) sts.

Work in garter st until piece measures 12 (12½, 13, 13½, 14, 14½) inches, ending with a WS row.

Divide for Armholes

Work across 38 (42, 46, 50, 54, 58) sts for right front, bind off 10 (12, 14, 16, 18, 20) sts, work across 77 (85, 93, 101, 109, 117) sts for back, bind off 10 (12, 14, 16, 18, 20) sts, then work across rem 38 (42, 46, 50, 54, 58) sts for left front.

Place back and right front sts on holders.

Left Front

Note: Read instructions before beginning as neck and armhole shaping is worked at the same time.

Shape Neck

Knit 1 row.

Dec 1 st at neck edge on next RS row, then [every other RS] row 16 (18, 19, 21, 22, 24) times. *At the same time*, shape armhole as follows:

Shape Armhole

Dec 1 st at armhole edge [every RS] row 4 (5, 7, 8, 10, 11) times, then [every other RS] row twice. When all left front shaping is complete—15 (16, 17, 18, 19, 20) sts.

Work even, if necessary, until armhole measures 8 (8½, 9, 9½, 10, 11) inches.

Place sts on holder. Cut yarn.

Back

Attach yarn to back, ready to work a WS row.

Continue in garter stitch, working armhole shaping as follows:

Shape Armholes

Dec 1 st at each armhole edge [every RS] row 4 (5, 7, 8, 10, 11) times, then [every other RS] row twice—65 (71, 75, 81, 85, 91) sts rem for back.

Work even until armhole measures 8 (8½, 9, 9½, 10, 11) inches.

Place sts on holder. Cut yarn.

Right Front

Note: Read instructions before beginning as neck and armhole shaping is worked at the same time.

Attach yarn to right front, ready to work a WS row.

Shape Neck

Knit 1 row.

Dec 1 st at neck edge on next RS row, then [every other RS] row 16 (18, 19, 21, 22, 24) times. *At the same time*, shape armhole as follows:

Shape Armhole

Dec 1 st at armhole edge [every RS] row 4 (5, 7, 8, 10, 11) times, then [every other RS] row twice. When all right front shaping is complete—15 (16, 17, 18, 19, 20) sts.

Work even, if necessary, until armhole measures 8 (8½, 9, 9½, 10, 11) inches.

Place sts on holder. Cut yarn.

Collar

With 2 strands of yarn held tog, cast on 232 (240, 248, 256, 264, 272) sts.

Work in Garter Drop St pat for approx 8 inches. Bind off all sts loosely.

Bottom Trim

With 2 strands of yarn held tog, cast on 192 (208, 224, 240, 256, 272) sts.

Work in Garter Drop St pat for approx 8 inches. Bind off all sts loosely.

Finishing

Block to measurements.

Using 3-needle bind-off (see page 29), join front shoulders to back shoulders from armhole edge toward center of garment. Bind off rem back neck sts.

Note: *It may be helpful to pin trim and collar in place before sewing to vest.*

Leaving the first and last 8 inches of the collar free, sew collar to vest beg at lower edge of right front bottom trim, along fronts and back neck and finishing at lower edge of left front bottom trim. Sew trim to vest bottom beg and ending 8 inches from trim edges, same as collar. Sew the 8 inches of unattached collar to the 8 inches of unattached trim on each side, forming draping points. •

T!P

Garter stitch is a reversible fabric, so either side can be the right side. Choose one side and mark it with a removable marker for easy reference when shaping or seaming.

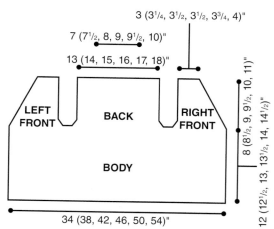

3 (3¼, 3½, 3½, 3¾, 4)"

7 (7½, 8, 9, 9½, 10)"

13 (14, 15, 16, 17, 18)"

8 (8½, 9, 9½, 10, 11)"

LEFT FRONT   BACK   RIGHT FRONT

BODY

12 (12½, 13, 13½, 14, 14½)"

34 (38, 42, 46, 50, 54)"

Note: Measurements are shown before trim is added.

Garter Ease

This quick-knit, drop-stitch cardigan is worked from side to side so you're not left with a bunch of fussy seams to sew later.

Gauge
14 sts and 26 rows = 4 inches/10cm in Garter Drop St pat.

To save time, take time to check gauge.

Note: As garment is worked from side to side, gauge should be measured with piece hanging sideways.

Special Abbreviations
Make 1 Left (M1L): Insert LH needle from front to back under strand between last st worked and next st on LH needle. With RH needle, knit through back of resulting loop.

Make 1 Right (M1R): Insert LH needle from back to front under strand between last st worked and next st on LH needle. With RH needle, knit into front of resulting loop.

Pattern Stitch
Garter Drop St

Row 1 (RS): Knit.

Row 2: Knit.

Row 3: *K1, yo; rep from * to last st, k1.

Row 4: Knit, dropping yo's without knitting them.

Rep Rows 1–4 for pat.

Pattern Notes
Circular needle is used to accommodate large number of stitches. Do not join; work back and forth in rows.

Use long-tail cast-on method throughout.

Increases and decreases are worked 1 st in from edge on Row 1 of pattern.

Left Sleeve
Cast on 40 (40, 42, 42, 44, 46) sts.

Knit 1 row.

Note: Work inc as follows: K1, M1R, work in Garter Drop St pat to last st, M1L, k1.

Beg Garter Drop St pat, inc 1 st each side on 5th row of pat, then [every 8 (4, 4, 4, 4, 4)] rows 6 (1, 3, 8, 8, 11) time(s), then [every 12 (8, 8, 8, 8, 8)] rows 2 (8, 7, 4, 4, 2) times, working inc sts into pat—58 (60, 64, 68, 70, 74) sts.

Work 7 more rows, ending with Row 4 of pat.

Left Shoulder
Cast on 42 (44, 46, 48, 49, 51) sts at beg of next 2 rows—142 (148, 156, 164, 168, 176) sts.

Work even for approx 6 (7, 7¾, 8½, 9¼, 9¾) inches, ending with a WS row.

Back

Work across first 71 (74, 78, 82, 84, 88) sts; place rem 71 (74, 78, 82, 84, 88) sts on holder for front.

Work in established Garter Drop St pat for 7 (7, 7½, 8, 8½, 9½) inches more, ending with a WS row.

Do not cut yarn.

Place sts on holder.

Left Front

With RS facing, transfer front sts to needles.

Join another ball of yarn and work in established Garter Drop St pat for 7 (7, 7½, 8, 8½, 9½) inches.

Loosely bind off all sts.

Right Front

Cast on 71 (74, 78, 82, 84, 88) sts.

Right Sleeve

Loosely bind off 42 (44, 46, 48, 49, 51) sts at beg next 2 rows—58 (60, 64, 68, 70, 74) sts.

Work 6 more rows.

Next row (Dec row): K1, ssk, work in pat to last 3 sts, k2tog, k1.

Rep Dec row [every 12 (8, 8, 8, 8, 8)] rows 1 (7, 6, 3, 3, 1) time(s), then [every 8 (4, 4, 4, 4, 4)] rows 7 (2, 4, 9, 9, 12) times—40 (40, 42, 42, 44, 46) sts.

Rep Rows 1–4 of Garter Drop St pat.

Knit 2 rows.

Loosely bind off all sts.

Finishing

Block pieces to measurements.

Sew underarm and side seams. ●

Knit 1 row.

Beg Garter Drop St pat and work for 7 (7, 7½, 8, 8½, 9½) inches, ending on same WS row as back.

Cut yarn.

Right Shoulder

With RS facing, place back sts on needle next to right front sts. Work across back sts, then front sts—142 (148, 156, 164, 168, 176) sts.

Work even in pat for 6 (7, 7¾, 8½, 9¼, 9¾) inches, ending with a Row 4 of pat.

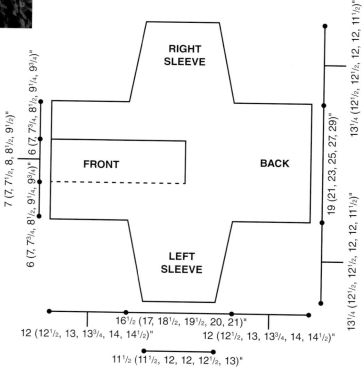

RIGHT SLEEVE

FRONT

BACK

LEFT SLEEVE

7 (7, 7½, 8, 8½, 9½)"

6 (7, 7¾, 8½, 9¼, 9¾)"

6 (7, 7¾, 8½, 9¼, 9¾)"

13¼ (12½, 12½, 12, 12, 11½)"

13¼ (12½, 12½, 12, 12, 11½)"

13¼ (12½, 12½, 12, 12, 11½)"

19 (21, 23, 25, 27, 29)"

16½ (17, 18½, 19½, 20, 21)"

12 (12½, 13, 13¾, 14, 14½)"

12 (12½, 13, 13¾, 14, 14½)"

11½ (11½, 12, 12, 12½, 13)"

Captivating Mesh Duo

This twinset will be a great complement to your wardrobe.
The pieces can be layered or simply worn individually.

Skill Level
 EASY

Sizes
Woman's small (medium, large, X-large, 2X-large, 3X-large)

Instructions are given for smallest size, with larger sizes in parentheses. When only 1 number is given, it applies to all sizes.

Finished Measurements
Jacket
Chest: 39 (43, 47, 51, 55, 59) inches
Length: 10 (11, 12, 13, 14, 15½) inches

Tank
Chest: 34½ (39, 43, 47, 51, 55) inches
Length (shorter side): 19½ (20½, 21½, 22½, 23½, 25) inches
Length (longer side): 21½ (22½, 23½, 24½, 25½, 27) inches

Materials
- Berroco Captiva (worsted weight; 60% cotton/23% polyester/17% acrylic; 98 yds/50g per hank): *for jacket:* 5 (6, 6, 7, 8, 9) hanks silver coin #5503; *for tank:* 6 (7, 8, 9, 10, 11) hanks silver coin #5503
- Size 7 (4.5mm) 32-inch circular needle or size needed to obtain gauge
- Stitch markers

For Jacket
- Size G/6 (4mm) crochet hook
- 1 (1-inch) button

Gauge
16 sts and 23 rows = 4 inches/10cm in Mesh pat for jacket.

18 sts and 26 rows = 4 inches/10cm in St st for tank.

To save time, take time to check gauge.

Special Abbreviations
Make 1 Left (M1L): Insert LH needle from front to back under strand between last st worked and next st on LH needle. With RH needle knit through back of resulting loop.

Make 1 Right (M1R): Insert LH needle from back to front under strand between last st worked and next st on LH needle. With RH needle knit into front of resulting loop.

Pattern Stitch
Mesh (multiple of 4 sts + 2)

Row 1 (RS): K1, *k2tog, [yo] twice, k2tog; rep from * to last st, k1.

Row 2: P1, *p2, k1, p1; rep from * to last st, p1.

Rep Rows 1 and 2 for pat.

Pattern Notes
Use long-tail cast-on method throughout.

A circular needle is used just to accommodate stitches for jacket. Do not join, work back and forth in rows.

Bind off all stitches loosely.

Jacket

Back
Cast on 78 (86, 94, 102, 110, 118) sts.

Purl 1 row.

Work in Mesh pat until back measures approx 2 (2½, 3, 3½, 4, 4½) inches, ending with a WS row.

Shape Armholes

Bind off 8 (12, 12, 12, 16, 16) sts at beg of next row, work in pat to last 8 (12, 12, 12, 16, 16) sts, knit rem sts omitting yo's—70 (74, 82, 90, 94, 102) sts.

Next row (WS): Bind off first 8 (12, 12, 12, 16, 16) sts, work across row—62 (62, 70, 78, 78, 86) sts.

Continue in Mesh pat until armholes measure approx 8 (8½, 9, 9½, 10, 11) inches.

Bind off all sts.

Place a marker approx 3¾ (3¾, 4¼, 4¾, 4¾, 5¼) inches in from each end of bound-off row.

Left Front

Cast on 38 (42, 46, 50, 54, 58) sts.

Purl 1 row.

Work in Mesh pat until front measures approx 2 (2½, 3, 3½, 4, 4½) inches, ending with a WS row.

Shape Armhole

Bind off 8 (12, 12, 12, 16, 16) sts at beg of next row—30 (30, 34, 38, 38, 42) sts.

Continue in Mesh pat until armhole measures approx 8 (8½, 9, 9½, 10, 11) inches.

Bind off all sts.

Right Front

Cast on 38 (42, 46, 50, 54, 58) sts.

Purl 1 row.

Work in Mesh pat until front measures approx 2 (2½, 3, 3½, 4, 4½) inches, ending with a WS row.

Next Row (RS): Work across row, omitting yo's over last 8 (12, 12, 12, 16, 16) sts.

Shape Armhole

Bind off 8 (12, 12, 12, 16, 16) sts at beg of next row—30 (30, 34, 38, 38, 42) sts.

Continue in Mesh St pat until armhole measures approx 8 (8½, 9, 9½, 10, 11) inches.

Bind off all sts.

Sleeves

Cast on 34 (34, 38, 38, 42, 42) sts.

Purl 1 row.

Note: Work inc rows on RS as follows: K1, M1R, work in Mesh pat to last st, M1L, k1.

Work in Mesh pat, inc 1 st each side of [5th (3rd, 3rd, 3rd, 3rd, 3rd) row] once, [every 6 (6, 6, 4, 4, 4)] rows 6 (17, 17, 7, 17, 22) more times, and then [every 8 (0, 0, 6, 6, 6)] rows 9 (0, 0, 12, 0, 2, 1) time(s)—66 (70, 74, 78, 82, 90) sts.

Work even in pat for approx 2½ (3½, 3½, 3½, 4½, 4½) more inches.

Bind off all sts.

Finishing

Block pieces to measurements.

Sew shoulder seams from shoulder edge to markers. Set in sleeves. Sew underarm and side seams.

Closure

With RS facing and crochet hook, attach yarn to lower corner of right front. Ch 10; sl st into edge of right front approx 1 inch above corner. Fasten off.

Sew button to lower corner of left front.

Optional
Fold back upper front neck edges and tack to make "lapel."

Tank
Cast on 25 (28, 31, 34, 37, 40) sts, pm to indicate right side seam, cast on 25 (28, 31, 34, 37, 40) sts.

Working back and forth in rows in St st, cast on 3 sts at end of next 16 rows—98 (104, 110, 116, 122, 128) sts.

Next row: Cast on 35 (42, 48, 54, 60, 66) sts, pm to indicate left side seam, cast on 35 (42, 48, 54, 60, 66) sts for remainder of body and join without twisting to work in rows—168 (188, 206, 224, 242, 260) sts.

Work to left side seam marker and mark as new beg of rnd.

****Working in rnds, knit 3 inches.

Dec rnd (RS): *K2tog, work St st to 2 sts before marker, ssk, sm; rep from * once.

Rep from ** twice more—156 (176, 194, 212, 230, 248) sts.

Work even until piece measures 11 (11½, 12, 12½, 13, 13½) inches from shortest (left side seam) edge.

Next rnd: *Work to 5 (7, 8, 9, 10, 12) sts before next marker, bind off 10 (14, 16, 18, 20, 24) sts; rep from * once more—68 (74, 81, 88, 95, 100) sts each for front and back.

Back
Beg with a WS row, work back and forth in St st on 68 (74, 81, 88, 95, 100) sts.

Dec 1 st by k1, ssk, work in St st to last 3 sts, k2tog, k1, [every RS row] 4 (5, 6, 7, 8, 9) times, then [every other RS row] twice—56 (60, 65, 70, 75, 78) sts.

Work even until armhole measures approx 7 (7½, 8, 8½, 9, 10) inches.

Bind off all sts.

Front
With WS facing, attach yarn to front, work back and forth in St st on these 68 (74, 81, 88, 95, 100) sts.

Dec 1 st each side [every RS row] 4 (5, 6, 7, 8, 9) times, then [every other RS row] twice—56 (60, 65, 70, 75, 78) sts.

When armhole shaping is complete, and ending with a WS row, beg neck shaping.

Shape Neck
Next row (RS): Knit across 19 (20, 22, 24, 26, 27) sts; join a 2nd ball of yarn and bind off center 18 (20, 21, 22, 23, 24) sts, knit rem sts—19 (20, 22, 24, 26, 27) sts on each side.

Working both sides at once with separate balls of yarn, dec 1 st at each neck edge [every RS row] 7 (7, 8, 9, 10, 10) times—12 (13, 14, 15, 16, 17) sts rem.

Work until armhole measures same as for back.

Bind off all sts.

Trim

Cast on 146 (162, 178, 194, 210, 226) sts.

Purl 1 row.

Work [Rows 1 and 2 of Mesh pat] 5 times.

Knit 2 rows.

Bind off all sts.

Finishing

Block pieces to measurements.

Sew shoulder seams.

Sew cast-on and bound-off edges of trim tog.
Sew trim to bottom of tank. ●

T!P

The stitch pattern is a short 2-row repeat and is easy to learn.

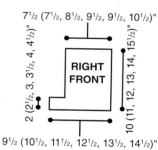

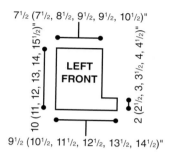

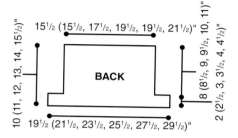

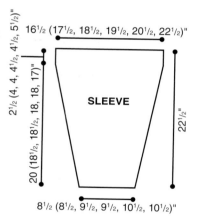

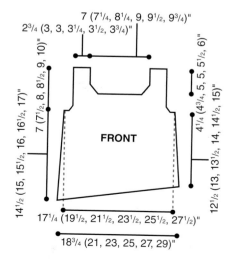

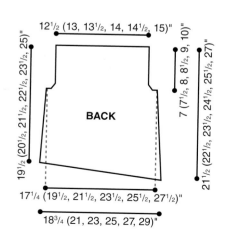

Meet the Designer

Kennita Tully is a widely published knitwear designer whose work has appeared in most knitting publications in the United States, including *Creative Knitting*, *Vogue Knitting*, *Knitter's Magazine*, *Better Homes and Gardens*, *Interweave Knits* and *Knit Simple*.

Kennita also owns and runs a yarn shop in Manhattan, Kan., where she teaches classes and workshops year-round. In addition, she self-publishes her own line of patterns under the name Wildflower knitwear.

Resources

Berroco Inc.
1 Tupperware Drive
Suite 4
North Smithfield, RI 02896-6815
(401) 769-1212
www.berroco.com

Habu Textiles
135 W. 29th St., Suite 804
New York, NY 10001
(212) 239-3546
www.habutextiles.com

Westminster Fibers
165 Ledge St.
Nashua, NH 03060
(800) 445-9276
www.westminsterfibers.com

General Information

Abbreviations & Symbols

[ ] work instructions within brackets as many times as directed

( ) work instructions within parentheses in the place directed

** repeat instructions following the asterisks as directed

* repeat instructions following the single asterisk as directed

" inch(es)

approx approximately
beg begin/begins/beginning
CC contrasting color
ch chain stitch
cm centimeter(s)
cn cable needle
dec(s) decrease/decreases/decreasing
dpn(s) double-point needle(s)
g gram(s)
inc(s) increase/increases/increasing

k knit
k2tog knit 2 stitches together
kfb knit in front and back
kwise knitwise
LH left hand
m meter(s)
M1 make one stitch
MC main color
mm millimeter(s)
oz ounce(s)
p purl
p2tog purl 2 stitches together
pat(s) pattern(s)
pm place marker
psso pass slipped stitch over
pwise purlwise
rem remain/remains/remaining
rep(s) repeat(s)
rev St st reverse stockinette stitch
RH right hand
rnd(s) rounds
RS right side

skp slip, knit, pass slipped stitch over—1 stitch decreased
sk2p slip 1, knit 2 together, pass slipped stitch over the knit 2 together—2 stitches decreased
sl slip
sl 1 kwise slip 1 knitwise
sl 1 pwise slip 1 purlwise
sl st slip stitch(es)
ssk slip, slip, knit these 2 stitches together—a decrease
st(s) stitch(es)
St st stockinette stitch
tbl through back loop(s)
tog together
WS wrong side
wyib with yarn in back
wyif with yarn in front
yd(s) yard(s)
yfwd yarn forward
yo (yo's) yarn over(s)

Skill Levels

BEGINNER

Beginner projects for first-time knitters using basic stitches. Minimal shaping.

EASY

Easy projects using basic stitches, repetitive stitch patterns, simple color changes and simple shaping and finishing.

INTERMEDIATE

Intermediate projects with a variety of stitches, mid-level shaping and finishing.

EXPERIENCED

Experienced projects using advanced techniques and stitches, detailed shaping and refined finishing.

Standard Yarn Weight System

Categories of yarn, gauge ranges and recommended needle sizes.

Yarn Weight Symbol & Category Names	0 LACE	1 SUPER FINE	2 FINE	3 LIGHT	4 MEDIUM	5 BULKY	6 SUPER BULKY
Type of Yarns in Category	Fingering 10-Count Crochet Thread	Sock, Fingering, Baby	Sport, Baby	DK, Light Worsted	Worsted, Afghan, Aran	Chunky, Craft, Rug	Super Chunky, Roving
Knit Gauge Range* in Stockinette Stitch to 4 inches	33–40 sts**	27–32 sts	23–26 sts	21–24 sts	16–20 sts	12–15 sts	6–11 sts
Recommended Needle in Metric Size Range	1.5–2.25mm	2.25–3.25mm	3.25–3.75mm	3.75–4.5mm	4.5–5.5mm	5.5–8mm	8mm and larger
Recommended Needle U.S. Size Range	000 to 1	1 to 3	3 to 5	5 to 7	7 to 9	9 to 11	11 and larger

* **GUIDELINES ONLY:** The above reflect the most commonly used gauges and needle sizes for specific yarn categories.

** Lace weight yarns are usually knitted on larger needles and hooks to create lacy, openwork patterns. Accordingly, a gauge range is difficult to determine. Always follow the gauge stated in your pattern.

Inches Into Millimeters & Centimeters

All measurements are rounded off slightly.

inches	mm	cm	inches	cm	inches	cm	inches	cm
⅛	3	0.3	5	12.5	21	53.5	38	96.5
¼	6	0.6	5½	14	22	56.0	39	99.0
⅜	10	1.0	6	15.0	23	58.5	40	101.5
½	13	1.3	7	18.0	24	61.0	41	104.0
⅝	15	1.5	8	20.5	25	63.5	42	106.5
¾	20	2.0	9	23.0	26	66.0	43	109.0
⅞	22	2.2	10	25.5	27	68.5	44	112.0
1	25	2.5	11	28.0	28	71.0	45	114.5
1¼	32	3.2	12	30.5	29	73.5	46	117.0
1½	38	3.8	13	33.0	30	76.0	47	119.5
1¾	45	4.5	14	35.5	31	79.0	48	122.0
2	50	5.0	15	38.0	32	81.5	49	124.5
2½	65	6.5	16	40.5	33	84.0	50	127.0
3	75	7.5	17	43.0	34	86.5		
3½	90	9.0	18	46.0	35	89.0		
4	100	10.0	19	48.5	36	91.5		
4½	115	11.5	20	51.0	37	94.0		

Knitting Basics

Long-Tail Cast-On

Leaving an end about an inch long for each stitch to be cast on, make a slip knot on the right needle.

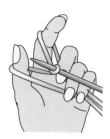

Place the thumb and index finger of your left hand between the yarn ends with the long yarn end over your thumb, and the strand from the skein over your index finger. Close your other fingers over the strands to hold them against your palm. Spread your thumb and index fingers apart and draw the yarn into a "V."

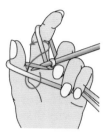

Place the needle in front of the strand around your thumb and bring it underneath this strand. Carry the needle over and under the strand on your index finger.

Draw through loop on thumb.

Drop the loop from your thumb and draw up the strand to form a stitch on the needle.

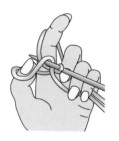

Repeat until you have cast on the number of stitches indicated in the pattern. Remember to count the beginning slip knot as a stitch.

Knit (K)

Insert tip of right needle from front to back in next stitch on left needle.

Bring yarn under and over the tip of the right needle.

Pull yarn loop through the stitch with right needle point.

Slide the stitch off the left needle. The new stitch is on the right needle.

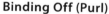

Purl (P)

With yarn in front, insert tip of right needle from back to front through next stitch on the left needle.

Bring yarn around the right needle counterclockwise. With right needle, draw yarn back through the stitch.

Slide the stitch off the left needle.

The new stitch is on the right needle.

Bind-Off

Binding Off (Knit)

Knit first two stitches on left needle. Insert tip of left needle into first stitch worked on right needle and pull it over the second stitch and completely off the needle.

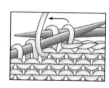

Knit the next stitch and repeat. When one stitch remains on right needle, cut yarn and draw tail through last stitch to fasten off.

Binding Off (Purl)

Purl first two stitches on left needle. Insert tip of left needle into first stitch worked on right needle and pull it over the second stitch and completely off the needle.

Purl the next stitch and repeat. When one stitch remains on right needle, cut yarn and draw tail through last stitch to fasten off.

Invisible Increase (M1)

There are several ways to make or increase one stitch.

Make 1 With Left Twist (M1L)

Insert left needle from front to back under the horizontal loop between the last stitch worked and next stitch on left needle.

With right needle, knit into the back of this loop.

To make this increase on the purl side, insert left needle in same manner and purl into the back of the loop.

Make 1 With Right Twist (M1R)

Insert left needle from back to front under the horizontal loop between the last stitch worked and next stitch on left needle.

With right needle, knit into the front of this loop.

To make this increase on the purl side, insert left needle in same manner and purl into the front of the loop.

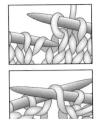

Decrease (Dec)

Knit 2 Together (K2tog)

Put tip of right needle through next two stitches on left needle as to knit. Knit these two stitches as one.

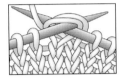

Purl 2 Together (P2tog)

Put tip of right needle through next two stitches on left needle as to purl. Purl these two stitches as one.

Centered Double Decrease (CDD)

Slip the next two stitches from the left needle to the right needle as if to knit two together.

Knit the next stitch on the left needle. Insert the left needle into the two slipped stitches and pull them over the first stitch and off the right needle.

Slip, Slip, Knit (Ssk)

Slip next two stitches, one at a time, as to knit from left needle to right needle.

Insert left needle in front of both stitches and knit them together.

Slip, Slip, Purl (Ssp)

Slip next two stitches, one at a time, as to knit from left needle to right needle. Slip these stitches back onto left needle keeping them twisted. Purl these two stitches together through back loops.

3-Needle Bind-Off

Use this technique for seaming two edges together, such as when joining a shoulder seam. Hold the edgestitches on two separate needles with right sides together.

With a third needle, knit together a stitch from the front needle with one from the back.

Repeat, knitting a stitch from the front needle with one from the back needle once more.

Slip the first stitch over the second.

Repeat knitting, a front and back pair of stitches together, then bind one off.

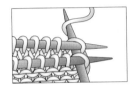

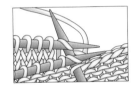

Crochet Stitches

. . . .

Chain (ch)

Yarn over, pull through loop on hook.

Chain Stitch

Slip Stitch (sl st)

Insert hook under both loops of the stitch, bring yarn over the hook from back to front and draw it through the stitch and the loop on the hook.

Slip Stitch

Single Crochet (sc)

Insert the hook in the second chain through the center of the V. Bring the yarn over the hook from back to front.

Draw the yarn through the chain stitch and onto the hook.

Again bring yarn over the hook from back to front and draw it through both loops on hook.

For additional rows of single crochet, insert the hook under both loops of the previous stitch instead of through the center of the V as when working into the chain stitch.

Single Crochet

Photo Index

5

9

13

19

Annie's® *Easy Openwork Knit Tops* is published by Annie's, 306 East Parr Road, Berne, IN 46711. Printed in USA. Copyright © 2013 Annie's. All rights reserved. This publication may not be reproduced in part or in whole without written permission from the publisher.

RETAIL STORES: If you would like to carry this pattern book or any other Annie's publications, visit AnniesWSL.com

Every effort has been made to ensure that the instructions in this pattern book are complete and accurate. We cannot, however, take responsibility for human error, typographical mistakes or variations in individual work. Please visit AnniesCustomerCare.com to check for pattern updates.

ISBN: 978-1-59635-741-9

1 2 3 4 5 6 7 8 9